THE BITTER
&
THE SWEET

THE BITTER
&
THE SWEET

The Saga of a
Black Family in America

Curtis L. Estes

REGENT PRESS
Berkeley, California
2021

ISBN 13: 978-1-58790-588-9

ISBN 10: 1-58790-588-4

Library of Congress Cataloging in Publication forthcoming

Printed in the United States of America

REGENT PRESS

Berkeley, California

www.regentpress.net

CONTENTS

FORWARD

I n 1967, at the age of 19, I was typical of those of my generation who hoped to change a world that, in our view, was too materialistic and lacked a sense of human values. I traveled to the South as a rebellious youth seeking adventure and escape from parental pressure.

I assumed, being from Chicago, that the human divide of Jim Crow was behind us. But after waking at a Greyhound station in Lexington, Kentucky, I found myself sternly rebuked by a fellow passenger: "Hey boy, where you going? Can't you see that bathroom is for coloreds?" When I looked up, sure enough, there was as sign that said "Colored bathroom and fountain." I was appalled. My view of the world's shortcomings took on a whole extra dimension at that moment.

Curtis Estes, at the age of 87, has lived half his life on the other side of that divide. When he honored me with an opportunity to edit his memoir I didn't hesitate to take on the task. Curtis is one of a handful of still-living individuals who has dwelled in a world where laws limited his ability to live his life freely. He was viewed by society not for his abilities or talents, but mainly by the color of his skin. This is a disadvantage that most White people only can imagine.

Over the last forty or so years there has been a new trend in our politics. Now laws are put in place to limit the voting rights of people of color, but the intent is hidden under a guise of equality. What many politicians say and what they actually do are not the same.

Despite generations of being held down solely because of race, Curtis and his family have been guided by optimism based on faith in themselves and their value as human beings. They have persisted in lifting themselves and living lives of dignity. They have been determined to attain training and education in pursuit of success regardless of the obstacles that others have put in their way. And despite the racism that still persists in our day, members of this family have continued to live with dignity and pursue their dreams.

I am grateful to Curtis for allowing me to experience – however vicariously – what it is like to see the world through his eyes. This is a story that, in my view, should be read and understood by everyone as a lesson for where we have been and where we might go when we believe in ourselves regardless of what others think. It also is a reminder about how far we yet have to go to genuinely create a society where all are seen and treated as equals.

It only slowly is dawning on us that those on both sides of the human divide suffer harm because of their disconnection to others – both emotionally and economically. Hopefully we will continue to move toward a world where each of us is recognized for who we are as individuals, with our talents and hopes, as equally valid members of the human family, where all understand that the only way to dignity for ourselves is to honor each other. The essence of democracy is that we thrive when we support everyone in developing their innate talents and abilities. This is a lesson we need to be reminded about every day.

— *Steve Zolno,*
Oakland, California,
August, 2021

INTRODUCTION

The most important reason for my memoir and research of the history of African-Americans and my family is to show how for four centuries, twelve million men, women and children from the African homeland changed forever the face and the character of our country. The enslavement of Africans was cruel, exploitative and dehumanizing. Slavery, which existed in many cultures, represents one of the longest and most sustained assaults on the life, integrity, and dignity of human beings.

This memoir also is about a family that has emphasized and strived for education. We always have believed that education would elevate and provide a better life for each of us as individuals and the family as a whole. An important part of education is learning from the past. Looking back at my life as a young man growing up on a farm in segregated Texas in the late 1940s, I wanted to know more about the history of African-Americans, and especially about my own family, which led me to years of research.

I started writing this memoir in the year 2000, over twenty years ago. I am now eighty-seven years old and feel that I must finish this project soon. For many years I was side-tracked by a busy life. Then, in 2016, while in the Berkeley, California, main library, I saw a notice about a writing workshop called the "Community Memoir Writing Project." Its aim was to guide people in how to write, reflect on their values, and share the stories of their lives. I immediately decided this is just what I needed. The class was led by founder/director Francis Lefkowitz, a person for whom I gained deep respect and admiration. There were twenty-five students in the class, and over a period of six weeks they wrote stories about their lives. Out of those, four stories were chosen by the head of acquisitions at UC Berkeley's Bancroft Library. My story, entitled "Plight," about growing up on a farm in segregated Texas, now is housed with the Mark Twain Papers. It is sitting in the same magnificent building that holds rare books, literary manuscripts, historical photographs, drawings, and documents.

I found that tracking down the educational history of African-Americans can present a challenge.

Few cultural groups face as many obstacles when it comes to researching their history. A lack of credible documentation can make the journey both difficult and time-consuming. Fortunately, a vast collection of resource materials now is available. Locating key information and records can often be done online or at the local library. My research also was made easier because of the Abstract of Title – a public record of family property rights – that has been in my family for four generations, dating back to January 18, 1842.

Many years ago, I read the biography of Dr. Carter G. Woodson, the "Father of Black History," a 1912 graduate of Harvard University. He stated that Black Americans must seek knowledge, working fervently and diligently for increased understanding of their background and heritage. This memoir is my attempt to do just that. As long as America turns away from history, and refuses to acknowledge the ongoing struggle of African-Americans, we will never be able to fully reckon with and repair the injustices of our own day.

Racism and discrimination toward African-Americans in the United States began during the colonial and slavery eras. One would think that after a long period of fighting for human rights, and the changes made by Constitutional Amendments, that discrimination would be behind us. But the issue continues to gain weight. Racism can be seen in modern socioeconomic inequality, including the educational system, employment, politics, law enforcement and housing. Racism is rooted in the reality that White people are often perceived to be superior, and Blacks relatively inferior.

This memoir is my attempt to bring together the story of five generations of my family with the reality of the Black experience in America. As I look over my long life I see that I have experienced the worst type of discrimination that America can offer and also have been blessed with a successful career, family and friends. Hopefully this memoir will be of interest to you, the reader, because of what it offers in lessons from the past and present, from which we hopefully can build a better future for ourselves and upcoming generations.

A BRIEF HISTORY OF BLACK AMERICA

THE BEGINNING OF SYSTEMIC RACISM IN AMERICA: THE WHITE LION, 1619

The first shipment of slaves from Africa to the Caribbean arrived in 1518.[1] In the area that eventually became the United States, slavery began with the occupation of Florida by the Spanish in the early 1500s. [2]

Jamestown, Virginia, founded in 1607, was the first English settlement in what became the U.S. In 1619, Jamestown was visited by a privateer sailing ship called the "White Lion." On board were several dozen Africans stolen from the Spanish slave ship San Juan Bautista, which was headed for Veracruz, New Spain (now part of Mexico). Some of the Africans were traded by the White Lion crew for food at Virginia's Point Comfort and placed in servitude. During this period Africans in the American colonies usually were treated as "servants," not slaves, just as were many White Europeans who had agreed to work three to seven years to pay for their passage to the New World. When the indentured servants' term of service expired, they were given a plot of land. Several free Africans bought servants of their own after they became land owners. Anthony H. Johnson, one of the original Jamestown Africans, is noted in the census records as one of the "largest holders of servants in the colony." [3]

For fifty years after the first cargo of Africans came to Jamestown, Virginia landlords imported more White servants than Africans. Not until 1661 was slavery officially recognized as legal in the Virginia colony. The colonists had realized the great potential of African labor. By the close of the century, Africans were being imported at the rate of 1,000 a year, and by 1715, when the White population of Virginia was 72,000, the Africans totaled 23,000. Over the next century, enslaved Africans and their offspring became the primary labor force supporting the cultivation of tobacco and cotton. Laws were passed at Jamestown which transformed an indentured form of servitude to one based upon race and lifetime enslavement. Slavery and systemic racism had come to America.

THE CONDITION OF THE SLAVE SHIPS

The slave ships were probably the most inhuman form of transportation for human beings to be devised until the Nazi freight lines began rolling toward the concentration camps of Eastern Europe during World War II. The African slaves were wedged below deck, chained to low-lying platforms, stacked in tiers with an individual space allotment that was six-feet long, sixteen inches wide, and perhaps three feet high. They were unable to stand erect or turn over. The slaves were given a twice daily ration of water plus either boiled rice, millet, cornmeal, or stewed yams in small portions, resulting in near starvation and attendant illnesses. Many Africans died or went mad during the long weeks at sea.

The loneliness, bewilderment and panic of those who survived the journey must have felt when they reached Boston, Baltimore or Charleston can hardly be imagined. The slaves were sick and exhausted, half naked, surrounded by sights of a strange civilization and the sound of a strange language. They were not allowed to talk to their fellow slaves. New arrivals who spoke the same African dialect were generally separated to keep them from conspiring to revolt.

Occasionally, some African captives success-
fully revolted and took over the ships. The most
famous incident occurred in 1839. A slave named
Joseph Cinque led a mutiny of 53 illegally purchased slaves on the Spanish slave ship Amistad,
killing the captain and two members of the crew.
They were vindicated by the U.S. courts in 1842
because slave transport was illegal and they were
allowed to return home.

When the ship carrying my great-grandfather
Anderson Estes as a crew member arrived in
Charleston, South Carolina, in 1835, the slaves were
docked and put in pens at Gadsden's Wharf, originally build in 1767, where an estimated 150,000
West African captives set foot on American soil.
Gadsden's Wharf was the primary point for slave
ships arriving in Charleston up until the banning of
slave imports at the end of 1807. Today, a substantial
number of African-Americans can trace an ancestor
to Charleston, the single largest point of entry for
African captives in North America. Countless men,
women, and children died at Gadsden's Wharf,
never reaching the auction block. Their freedom
was stolen, their names forgotten, their histories cut
short, and their stories forever left untold.

Many of the slaves who arrived at Gadsden's

Wharf were sold at auction and brought to a plantation known as Somerset Place in North Carolina. Somerset Place was one of the South's largest slaveholding plantations, located on the shore of Lake Phelps. The labor needs of that plantation dictated the number of slaves needed to perform certain tasks. At the beginning, the work force included 167 enslaved men, women, and children varying in skills. Mostly, they were young, strong men in their late teens and early twenties. Some young women worked beside them planting and harvesting crops, but hard tasks such as uprooting tree stumps and hauling mud away from the ditches were seen as "men's work."

Three generations of the Collins family owned the plantation over its 80-year tenure from 1785 to 1865. Over its history more than 860 enslaved people, two free Black employees and around 50 White employees lived and labored on the 100,000-acres, producing rice, corn, and wheat. For each slave house, the family would be issued three and one-half pounds of sawed up pork per week, milk, flour, rice, and molasses. They supplemented their diets with fish from the lake, while trapping small animals like rabbits and raccoons.

The sailors on Portuguese slave ships were

often badly paid and subject to brutal discipline. While conditions for the crew were vastly better than those of the enslaved people, they remained harsh, and contributed to a high death rate. Malaria and yellow fever were the most frequent causes of death among sailors. A high crew mortality rate on the return voyage was in the captain's interest, as it reduced the number of sailors who had to be paid on reaching home port. Crew members who survived the trip back to Portugal were frequently cheated out of their wages.

With this thought in mind, my great-grandfather, Anderson Estes, a Portuguese crew member, decided to abandon ship and traveled from Charleston to San Antonio, Texas. He joined the Texas Militia in August of 1836, after the "Battle of the Alamo," under the command of General Sam Houston. Sam Houston had already served in the U.S. House of Representatives and as governor of Tennessee when he moved to Texas in 1832. Houston emerged as a leader among the settlers, and in 1835, he was chosen commander and chief of the Texas Army.

THE SLAVE AUCTIONS

In Charleston, auctions were advertised when it was known that a slave ship was due to arrive. Posters were displayed around the town. When a slave ship docked, the slaves would be taken off and placed in a pen. They would be washed and their skin covered with grease, or sometimes tar, to make them look healthier so they would fetch as much money as possible. They would also be branded with a hot iron to identify them as slaves.

There were two main types of slave auctions: 1. Those where they were sold to the highest bidder, and 2. "Grab and Go."

Highest Bidder: The slaves would be brought from the pen, in turn, to stand on a raised platform so they could be seen by the buyers. Before the bidding began, buyers could come onto the platform to inspect the slaves closely. The slaves had to endure being poked, plodded and forced to open their mouths for the buyers. The auctioneer would decide a price to start the bidding. It would be higher for fit, young slaves, and lower for older, very young or sickly slaves. Potential buyers would then bid against each other. The person who bid the most would then own the slave.

Grab and Go: People who wanted to buy a slave on the day of the auction would pay the trader an agreed amount of money. The trader would then give them a ticket for each slave they bought. At the sound of the drum roll, the door to the slave pen would be opened and the buyers would rush in and grab the slave or slaves they wanted. The buyer then checked their slaves out by returning their tickets to the slave trader.

The slave owners had total control over their slaves, often forcing them into hard, painful, and dangerous work. Slaves were not allowed to strive for their own goals. For many, their days consisted of slaughtering animals, digging ditches, cutting wood and bringing it back to the house, driving the owners where they wanted to go, planting and harvesting crops, and performing repairs that needed to be done on the plantation. If they refused, they were beaten.

Slaves did not receive proper nutrition, especially for the physical tasks that they performed. They worked all day and into the night without receiving well-rounded meals; thus their immune systems were poor. The treatment of enslaved people in the United States varied by time and place, but was generally brutal. Whipping and rape were routine, but usually not in front of White outsiders or even the plantation owner's family. One slave owner said, "when I whip niggers, I take them out of sight and hearing of the house, and no one in the family knows it." [4]

On September 22, 1862, toward the beginning of the Civil War, Lincoln issued a preliminary emancipation proclamation, and on January 1, 1863, he made it official that "slaves within any state, or designated part of a state — in rebellion — shall be then, thenceforward, and forever free."

JIM CROW, SEGREGATION, AND WHITE SUPREMACY, 1877-1965

During a period called Reconstruction, after the Civil War from 1865 to 1877, the rights of Black Americans in the South were supposed to be guaranteed under the supervision of the U.S. Government. But when Reconstruction ended, White southerners began a system of blatant racism and White supremacy. Just as under the slave system, Black men and women were treated as inferior. Several White organizations, including the Ku Klux Klan, were founded as a means of keeping Blacks "in their place." Many so-called "Christians" also preached hatred and racism as many still do today. [5] This systemic racism was enforced through terrorist activities like cross burning and lynching, as well as by "separate but equal" facilities, including schools, that were far from equal.

The US Supreme Court decision, in *Brown v. Board of Education,* on May 17, 1954, forced the desegregation of public schools in 21 states. This encouraged and empowered many who felt for the first time that they had a "friend" in the court. The strategy of education, lobbying, and litigation that had defined the Civil Rights Movement up to that point broadened to include an emphasis on "direct action." This included boycotts, sit-ins, freedom rides, marches, and other tactics that relied on mass mobilization, nonviolent resistance, and civil disobedience.

A century after the Civil War, resistance to the lingering racism and discrimination that began during the slavery era led to the Civil Rights movement of the 1960s and Civil Rights Act of 1964, which achieved the greatest political and social gains for Black Americans since Reconstruction.

THE ORIGIN OF HISTORICALLY
BLACK COLLEGES AND UNIVERSITIES

Black colleges and universities were established to serve the educational needs of Black Americans. Prior to the time of their establishment, and for many years afterwards, Blacks were generally denied admission to traditional White institutions. As a result, HBCUs (Historically Black Colleges and Universities) became the principal means for providing postsecondary education to Black Americans. After the Civil War, two organizations, The American Missionary Association (AME) and the Freedmen's Bureau, helped African-Americans establish Black clerics and provide a Christian education for Blacks. Southern institutions, segregated schools that largely depended on White philanthropy to exist, focused on industrial education that would prepare them for subservient roles in society. These institutions were, in most cases, academically inferior to their White counterparts.

The institute for "Colored Youth," the first higher education institution for Blacks, was founded in Cheyney, Pennsylvania, in 1837. It was followed by two other Black institutions, Lincoln University in Pennsylvania (1854), and Wilberforce University in Ohio (1856). Although they were called "universities" or "institutes" at the beginning, a major part of their mission in the early years was to provide elementary and secondary schooling for students who had no previous education. It was not until the early 1900s that HBCUs began to offer courses and programs at the postsecondary level.

The federal Morrill Acts were designed to force former confederate states to "show that race was not an admissions criterion, or else designate a separate land-grant institution for persons of color." The first Morrill Act legislation was passed in 1862, and was the start of the land grant system of providing degrees outside of private universities. The Morrill Act would give "states public lands provided the lands be sold or used for profit and the proceeds to establish at least one college — hence, land grant colleges — that would teach agriculture and the mechanical arts." This act would spawn many of the public state institutions that are still in existence today like Clemson University, University of Georgia, Texas A&M, and the University of Wisconsin, to name a few. The second Morrill Act of 1890 would spawn the creation of almost half of the existing public 4-year HBCUs, which, since their inception, have produced changemakers who have altered the globe. This is something that should rightfully be celebrated, but it also should be acknowledged that these schools were designed to control and constrict Black education.

The growth of HBCUs spurred controversy among prominent African-Americans in the late 19th and early 20th centuries. Some critics noted that many, particularly those existing in the years immediately following the Civil War, were founded by Whites, some of whom had negative preconceptions of the social, cultural, and intellectual capabilities of Blacks.

Because the doors of American universities are more open to Blacks now than in the past, a vast number of Black students are enrolled at predominantly White institutions. Nevertheless, HBCUs continue to pull their weight as producers of Black graduates in many disciplines, such as science and engineering, that are vital to the nation's future. A few famous graduates of HBCUs include W.E. DuBois, Martin Luther King, Kamala Harris, David Dinkins, Jessie Jackson, Spike Lee, Toni Morrison, Thurgood Marshal, Jerry Rice, Langston Hughes, and Lionel Richie. These institutions educate and train many minority graduates, who go on to productive and successful careers in large part because they prepare them in nurturing and supportive environments. Many of these institutions have proven successful at educating first-time and low-income students.

To better understand the status of Blacks in education between the years 1950-1975, one must have an understanding of the historical events that shaped that period. Since the days of slavery, constraining Black education was used to quell fears of equality among Whites. But this only intensified Black people's desire for education. After emancipation, Black education was relegated to poorly funded, segregated schools.

Education has shown us time after time that it can succeed in breaking old cycles of poverty, chains of discrimination, and limited opportunities for some of society's most maligned and marginalized groups. But as exciting as is this belief in education as the great equalizer, it very often is difficult to obtain for those who are struggling to maintain life's basic needs.

Black Americans have made progress since the 1940s. We can see a fuller picture of the role that education played for certain groups. As Jim Crow Laws that enforced segregation were challenged — in the courts and on the streets — America's educational institutions were still slow to change. Most elite colleges and universities were willing to disregard the constitution to keep Blacks "in their place."

Racism and discrimination still are facts of life for many Black Americans. Studies show that Black college students report higher levels of stress related to racial discrimination than other racial or ethnic groups. The unfortunate reality is that many Black Americans experience subtle and overt discrimination from preschool all the way through college.

The 1960s was a time of great turmoil and social unrest in America and in the Black community. At this time, Blacks began to attend predominately White institutions at an increasing rate. But toward the end of the decade, more Blacks were choosing to attend Historically Black Colleges and Universities. Sociologist Jacqueline Fleming discovered that while many Black students chose White institutions because of better academic reputations, financial aid, and academic resources superior to those of Black colleges, the presence of racism or a hostile environment impedes progress for many Blacks. Fleming's studies show that Black students tend to perform better and exhibit more personal growth at historically Black institutions. [6]

Black History Month is a time to revisit

America's past and honor the achievements of Black Americans. We must recognize that Black history is part of everyone's history. Black educational attainment should be one of the accomplishments we celebrate each year because it honors and confirms what is possible.

The legacy of slavery is a fundamental contradiction in our country's history that nearly tore it apart. African-American history is not all about slavery, but slavery had a profound impact and reach that continues today. Dr. Carter G. Woodson, the founder of what started out as Black History Week, hoped that one day the need for such a special designation would disappear; that the history and contributions of Black people would be fully embedded in our history and curriculum. W.E.B. DuBois wrote, "the problem of the 20th century is the problem of the color-line." But in the 21st century, so far, the problem persists. Slavery, segregation and discrimination, particularly against voters of color, informs American history up to the present day. Half of our country was built with slave labor, and we went to war over slavery, but we have not yet made good on our nation's founding principle: *"That all men are created equal, that they are endowed by their Creator with certain unalienable*

Rights, that among these are Life, Liberty and the pursuit of Happiness." [7] None of us can truly be free unless equal treatment is not just a promise, but an actuality, for all Americans.

OKLAHOMA RACE MASSACRE OF 1921

Oklahoma became a state in 1907. During the ensuing thirteen years more than two dozen Blacks were lynched in the state. Tulsa itself was segregated, and the use of public facilities, such as restrooms and drinking fountains, were racially restricted.

The Tulsa neighborhood of Greenwood was a prospering area, almost entirely populated by Blacks in 1921. Tulsa underwent an oil boom in the early 20th century, and as the city prospered, the Greenwood area also flourished. Hotels, banks, grocery stores, haberdasheries, and other forms of commerce catered to, and were owned by, Blacks, offering opportunities and services which were denied them by White-owned facilities and businesses.

Racial segregation restricted personal relationships with White women, other than working for them, and even commercial interaction was eyed suspiciously by some Whites. An accusation by a

White man or a White woman against a Black person nearly always led to a conviction, as Blacks were denied the right to sit on juries (only registered voters could be jurors). The fear of White lynch mobs was present in Tulsa as well as in the rest of the South. Racial tensions were high, both from the news of riots across the U.S. during the summer of 1919 (known as the Red Summer riots) and from the competition for jobs after the First World War.

On May 30, 1921, Dick Rowland, a young African-American shoe shiner, was accused of assaulting a White elevator operator named Sarah Page in the elevator of a building in downtown Tulsa. The next day the *Tulsa Tribune* printed a story saying that Rowland had tried to rape Page, with an accompanying editorial stating that a lynching was planned for that night. That evening mobs of both African Americans and Whites descended on the courthouse where Rowland was being held. When confrontation between an armed African-American man and a White protester resulted in the death of the latter the White mob was incensed, and the Tulsa Massacre was ignited.

Over the next two days, mobs of White people looted and set fire to African-American businesses and homes throughout the city. Many of the mob members were recently returned World War I veterans trained in the use of firearms and are said to have shot African-Americans on sight. Some survivors even claimed that people in airplanes dropped incendiary bombs. White residents who were deputized and given weapons by the city officials attacked Black residents.

The massacre left between 30 and 300 people dead, mostly African-Americans, and destroyed Tulsa's prosperous Black neighborhood. More than 1400 homes and businesses were burned, and nearly 10,000 people were left homeless. Despite its severity and destructiveness, the Tulsa race massacre was barely mentioned in history books until the late 1900s, when a state commission was formed to document the incident. Almost immediately afterwards there were efforts to figuratively sweep the incident under the rug.

The Tulsa Tribune, which published the inflammatory editorial suggesting the existence of a plan to lynch Dick Rowland, is long defunct and paper copies of its edition for that day are non-existent. The microfilm copy is of a newspaper with the editorial page partially torn out. The actual words of the newspaper which incited some in the crowd are not available to historians.

Due to the persistence of African-American civil rights leaders like Martin Luther King Jr., President John F. Kennedy pushed for the Civil Rights act which became law under Lyndon Johnson in 1964. The Civil Rights Act ended segregation in public places and banned employment discrimination on the basis of race, color, religion, sex or national origin.

Over 150 years after emancipation and the right to freedom and equal treatment was established in our country, African-Americans are still attempting to be treated as equals in many places. Systemic racism in the state of Oklahoma and many areas of the country continues.

Driving as an African-American is sometimes a nightmare due to discrimination and harassment by police. In 1998, 35 years after the Civil Rights Act, U. S. Army Sergeant Rossano V. Gerald and his son were driving through Oklahoma. During this drive they were stopped twice, and were greatly harassed during their second stop. Not only did the stop last approximately two and a half hours, but they were locked in a car with fans blowing hot air and no air conditioning. They were told if they tried to escape, the dogs would attack. No person of color is generally safe from these acts of harassment. Nothing matters: being a law-abiding citizen with a good job, the type of vehicle, one's age, or which part of the country one lives, as long as a person's skin tone is Black or brown, that person may be subjected to this kind of treatment. [8]

CONTINUED SYSTEMIC RACISM

Ongoing incidents of systemic racism in the U.S. has had and still has psychological effects on African-Americans. In 1955, Emmett Till, a 14-year-old African American, was falsely accused of flirting with Carolyn Bryant, a White woman, while visiting his relatives in Mississippi. Emmett went to the Bryant store with his cousins and allegedly whistled at Carolyn. Her husband Roy Bryant, and brother-in-law J. W. Milam, kidnapped and brutally murdered Emmett, dumping his body in the Tallahatchie River. Bryant and Milam were acquitted for this gruesome murder, which outraged the African-American community nationwide.

The newspaper coverage and murder trial galvanized a generation of young African-Americans to join the Civil Rights Movement out of fear that such an incident could happen to friends, family, or themselves. Many interviewees in the Civil Rights

History Project have stated how this case deeply affected their lives psychologically and still affects the lives of African-Americans.

Sisters Joyce and Dorie Ladner, who grew up in Mississippi, remember keeping a scrapbook of every article about Till, and they feared that their brothers could be killed too. Dorie Ladner was inspired to learn more about the law after Bryant and Milam were acquitted: "That's where the light bulb went off; why aren't they being punished? And that's when I went on my quest to try to understand the whole legal system and equal rights and justice under the law." Joyce Ladner, who has written a number of books on Black issues, discussed how she coined the term, "Emmett Till Generation," which she used to describe the African-American baby boomers in the South who were inspired by Till's murder to join a burgeoning movement of mass meetings, sit-ins, and marches to demand equal treatment under the law. [9]

The long history of systemic racism continues in America. Prior to, and since this incident, countless other cases of blatant discrimination and attacks on Blacks have occurred. Police kill about 1,000 people in the U.S. annually and about half are young Black men, the vast majority 20-40 years of age, although only about 13 percent of the population is Black. [10]]

Police in the U.S. kill at approximately 100 times the rate of police in other industrial countries. In recent years there has been a long list of Black men and women killed as a result of either police action or racist hate crimes: Oscar Grant, Tony Robinson, Tony McDade, Travon Martin, Michael Brown, Eric Garner, Tamir Rice, Sean Reed, Yassin Mohamed, Ahmaud Arbery, Breonna Taylor, Philando Castile, Alton Sterling, and George Floyd, who died under the knee of a police officer in 2020. These are among many high-profile cases.

The difference today is that everyone carries a portable video camera in their smart phone. In many cases we see that the official police report falsely describes an incident, which begs the question as to how much systemic discrimination goes uncaptured on video. In many respects it appears that Jim Crow, segregation, and violence against Blacks have returned and indeed were encouraged by the administration of Donald Trump (2017-2021). Beyond these overt results of discrimination, African-American men and women have been disproportionately imprisoned due to unequal law enforcement and sentencing practices. Employment discrimination increases the risk of poverty.

Systemic racism, poverty, and injustice have led to significantly higher risks of death and disease. [11]

THE ONGOING EFFECTS OF SLAVERY

Although slavery in the United States has been abolished for many years, ongoing psychological and emotional stress continues for African-Americans who still struggle to deal with the traumatic effects of discrimination. The incidents presented in the previous paragraphs have affected the psyche of the average Black person living in the United States. During slavery, Africans were traumatized, terrorized, stigmatized, and abused by slave-owners in order to invoke fear into the hearts and minds of people kidnapped from their country, brought to the New World, and forced into a dismal life of exploitation, repression and rape. One also must consider and understand the psychological pain Black people still experience in a society that continues to discriminate against them. The abuse from the past has caused Black people to internalize racism and oppression and has created a legacy of separation within American society.

Professor Heidi J. Nast, of DePaul University, in her 2004 paper, states that after the Oklahoma Massacre, the deliberate burning down of a town, businesses, and the killing of citizens, was ignored or suppressed into the unconscious. In the public consciousness it seemed that it did not exist. The neglect of communication about what happened to African-Americans during and after slavery leaves Black people to harvest the effects of tragedies that happened to their ancestors. By harvesting the pain and trauma, the Black American or the "bestial being" within as Nast describes it, continues to be repressed. Nast also states, "the voicelessness from the events that happened during slavery still has not been addressed openly and to the fullest extent, therefore African-Americans are still affected by that pain." [12]

Psychologists Michael Flynn and Charles B. Strozier express a view about how much victims can remember. When people are psychologically traumatized they may have a lapse of memory because the event was so stressful, and the pieces of those memories are non-chronological. The torture and abuse that African slaves went through have been so painful that the history/memory of slavery and racism cannot be explained or understood clearly by them. According to these authors, African-Americans were traumatized to the point where their history has some missing pieces, and many African-Americans today are suffering from post-traumatic-stress disorder because they still feel the effects

33

of slavery which has not been outwardly and remorse-fully addressed by White America. Flynn and Strozier also state, "we focus more on the victim than the perpe-trator. If America can actually discuss slavery and how a race was traumatized to the point where they are still psychologically suffering today by internalizing racism and oppression, then it will begin the healing process for African Americans." [13]

Chapter 1

Origin of the Estes family

y mother passed away in 1986. She had in her possession an Abstract of Title. This is a description of the land given to Anderson Estes, my great-grandfather, by the President of the Republic of Texas, Sam Houston, for fighting with him to gain independence from Mexico in 1836. This Abstract of Title has been in my family for five generations, dating back to January 18, 1842.

Dr. Carter G. Woodson Woodson was convinced that "if a race has no recorded history, it has no worthwhile tradition. It becomes a negligible factor in the thought of the world, and it stands in danger of being exterminated."[11] He also believed: "We should emphasize not Negro History, but the Negro in History. What we need is not a history of selected races or nations, but the history of the world, void of national bias, race hate, and religious prejudice. There should be no indulgence in undue eulogy of

35

THE BITTER & THE SWEET

the Negro. The case of the Negro is well taken care of when it has shown how he has influenced the development of civilization."

From the beginning, education for African slaves in this country was nearly nonexistent, especially in the years before the Civil War. They were considered to be cargo or chattel to be bought, sold or traded. Our ancestors had to survive tremendous physical and mental torture that no ordinary human being could be expected to withstand. Brilliant and beautiful minds were wasted under the whip or behind the plow. Blacks interested in learning had to receive their education under cover of darkness and threats of violence, and very few had the benefit of a formal school education.

The African-American has played a vital part in the building of America's economic strength: as a fighting man in all of this country's wars, as a contributor to national culture, as a figure of importance in sports, and as a participant in all of the varied activities of American life. All across America, although we have a deep appreciation of history, we haven't always had a deep appreciation of each other's history. What is true in the South and the North is true for America. We must understand that justice grows out of the recognition of ourselves in each other, that liberty for any of us depends on everyone being free. History can't be a weapon to justify injustice, or a shield against progress, but must be a manual for how to avoid repeating the mistakes of the past, and a means to break our vicious cycle of violence against each other. The path of grace involves an open mind, but more importantly, an open heart!

Motivated by both the words of Dr. Woodson, and the Abstract of Title that my mother left me, I started to research my family's history on April 18, 2000, at the Oakland Family History Center. This is a branch of the Family History Library of the Church of Jesus Christ of Latter-Day Saints in Salt Lake City, Utah.

I found that my great-grandfather Anderson Estes, a native of Portugal, born between the years 1800 and 1810, was a crew member on a Portuguese slave ship. The transatlantic slave trade began in the 16th century when Portuguese interests in Africa moved away from the fabled deposits of gold to a much more readily available commodity — enslaved people. By the 17th century the trade was in full swing, reaching a peak toward the end of the 18th century.

The principal region of slave purchase was

West Central Africa. During the early years of the slave trade, the Portuguese purchased Africans who had been taken as slaves during tribal wars. As the demand for slaves grew, the Portuguese began to enter the interior of Africa to forcibly take captives.

In 1444, an expedition of six Portuguese ships under Henry the Navigator sailed to islands off the coast of western Africa and seized 235 men, women and children, separating families and causing great distress among those captured. A court chronicler described the scene: Some held their heads low, their faces bathed in tears...some groaned very piteously, looking toward the heavens fixedly and crying aloud, as if they were calling on the father of the universe to help them; others struck their faces with their hands and threw themselves on the ground. [12]

The African trade, together with the prosperity of the Cape Verde islands, expanded greatly with the development of labor-intensive plantations growing sugar, cotton, and tobacco in the Caribbean and America. The Portuguese had a monopoly of the transport of the African slaves to their own colony of Brazil, but other nations with transatlantic interests soon became visitors to the slave coast.

Texas independence occurred in 1836 when Texan forces defeated Mexican General Antonio

Lopez de Santa Anna. The conflict between Texas and Mexico lasted from late 1835 to May 1836. After the battle of San Jacinto, Sam Houston became the President of the Republic of Texas. To honor the soldiers who fought with him to gain their independence from Mexico, he gave them a portion of land for their services. According to the "Abstract of Title" that has been in my family for five generations, recorded in book "R", page 18, Deed, Records of Lee County, Texas #764, The State of Texas to Anderson Estes:

I, Sam Houston, President of the Republic of Texas aforesaid, by virtue of the power vested in me by law, and in accordance with the status of said Republic in such case made and provided do by these presents grant to Anderson Estes, his heirs and assigns forever one league of twenty-five million square varas of land, situated and described as follows: In Washington County, South of the Yegua, known on the map of said county as league "M."

In today's land measures, the amount of land that was given to Anderson was 157 acres. The present location is near Giddings, Texas, the county seat of Lee County, located 55 miles east of Austin. Its population was 5,665 in the 2010 census.

My sister Edna, a retired school teacher, lived

until her recent death at age 92 in Giddings. In 2016, during our family reunion, relatives from all over the United States and other countries attended there. My two sons, Curtis and Jonathan went with me. It was the first time they had seen these relatives, and they were delighted to meet them.

In 1843, my great-grandfather built his home on the 157 acres of land. He started raising cotton and tobacco which were the most productive and lucrative products at that time. Later, he met and married a local woman named Elizabeth Wilson. From this marriage there were two or three children born. Their names are unknown.

Anderson engaged in several years of farming with the help of the local white residents who were his only source of labor and who were not able to purchase their own land. After purchasing many more acres, his labor force was not large enough to sustain and maintain the products that the newly bought acreage could produce. Anderson purchased a few slaves at the auction market, but the exact number of slaves he purchased is unknown.

According to my research his purchase of slaves consisted of at least three girls between thirteen and seventeen. I was not able to find any information regarding these three enslaved girls. I am not sure if they were recently enslaved, or if they were the first or second generation of enslaved girls; nor do I know what area of Africa they were from. But one thing is certain, one of the enslaved girls (name unknown) and the slave owner, Anderson Estes, had a son named Roland Estes in 1843, who was my grandfather.

During the eighteenth century many of the American slave owners were having problems with their slaves. Some of the problems were uprisings, running away, crops left in the field too long for maximum profit, occasional fires, and the animals that were killed intentionally by the slaves. In December of 1712, the slave owners of Virginia sent for a British slave owner named Willie Lynch who lived in the West Indies to come and teach them about slave ownership. Willie Lynch delivered his speech to the slave owners on the bank of the James River in the Colony of Virginia. The term "lynching" is derived from his last name. Willie Lynch is the author of the book, *The Making of a Slave.*

I am not sure if Anderson Estes believed in the doctrine of Willie Lynch, but he did own slaves. As I read the history and the life of Anderson Estes, it was impossible to determine if he was a ruthless slave owner or had some compassion for his slaves.

Nevertheless, this is my memoir of the Estes family, that includes my great-grandfather the slave owner and his descendants, who currently are the following families: Huff, McNeil, Taylor, Griffin, and Kerr and possibly others I may not know off. The plight of the African in America has been hard and often unbearable.

On January 1, 1863, President Abraham Lincoln signed and issued the Emancipation Proclamation. It declared that "all persons held as slaves within the rebellious states are, and henceforward shall be, free." The Proclamation announced the acceptance of Black men into the Union army and navy, enabling the liberated to become liberators. By the end of the Civil War, 170,000 Black soldiers and sailors had fought for the Union and for freedom. [13]

The 14th Amendment of the United States Constitution (1868) declared that: "All persons born or naturalized in the United States, and subject to the jurisdiction thereof, are citizens of the United States and of the state wherein they reside." The 15th Amendment (1870) was passed to guarantee African-American men the right to vote. But women, Black and white, were not allowed to vote nationwide until 1920, after the passage of the 19th Amendment.

I will now reflect on the life story of my grand-father, Roland Estes. Roland was allowed to live in the house with the children of Anderson and his wife Elizabeth. He learned to read and write and was able to read many books on a great number of subjects. He was also taught how to transact and manage the farm business. His level of education probably was comparable to the average white person of that time.

In 1860, at the age of seventeen, Roland was given his freedom papers, but he was still not considered by many a free man because emancipation had not been declared. Roland remained free during the Civil War years 1860-1865, although slavery was not abolished until 1863. It is possible that since his father Anderson Estes had a great amount of influence within the community that white people respected his decision that Roland would remain free.

In 1875, at the age of thirty-two, Roland lived and owned property in the community of Post Oak, Lee County, Texas. He married a young ex-slave named Jennifer Kerr, and they had eight children, with my father Ira Lucas Estes, born 1902, being the youngest. Roland was able to acquire many acres of land, but he did not farm as most of the people in that area did. The people of that community raised mostly cotton and corn. Cotton was their main product for sale on the market, and corn was mostly used for personal consumption and livestock.

Roland became involved in the business of producing molasses. He grew sugar cane, which he used to produce his molasses. He sold and distributed molasses throughout the Post Oak Community until his death at the age of fifty-three in 1896. After the death of Roland, my grandmother Jennifer became the matriarch of the Estes family.

The address of the property that my grandparents owned was Route 1, Box 36, Ledbetter, Texas. My father Ira was born and raised in this house. After the death of my grandfather, my father remained in this home with my grandmother. At the age of thirty, my father married my mother, Ella Jones Estes, the daughter of William and Sarah Jones, who lived in the Jones Colony located approximately ten miles from the Post Oak Community. I was born in this home on April 6, 1934, delivered by a midwife and my mother's sister, my Aunt Amanda. My grandmother died several years later. My father, mother and I lived in this house until they separated and divorced in 1945.

Chapter 2

Home and School

I am the only child of Ira Lucas Estes and Ella Jones Estes, although I did have a half-sister. My father had been married before and he had a daughter named Edna. We did not live in the same household. She lived with her grandparents in a nearby community, but we saw each other quite often and were very close.

My family and I lived in the same house as my grandparents. Our farmhouse was located in a rural community named Post Oak, in Lee County, Texas, approximately fifty-five miles South of Austin.

Our home had no electricity or running water, nor did we have an indoor toilet. If we had any reading or writing to do, it had to be done during daylight hours. We used kerosene lamps and lanterns for light, but they were not sufficient for reading and writing. My mother would often remind me to do my homework before dark.

On our farm we raised mostly cotton, corn and

a variety of vegetables. We did not own any modern farm equipment during that time; no tractors, cultivators or cotton-picking machines. All of the work was done manually. At the age of nine, I knew how to make furrows in the soil with a horse- drawn plow. I could hoe, pick cotton, cut wood for the kitchen stove and the fireplace, and feed the many animals that we had on the farm, that included chickens, turkeys, horses, cows and pigs. I was the only child and automatically these chores were all mine.

Our cotton was sold at the local gin in Giddings, Texas, which was approximately fifteen miles from the farm. The cotton was usually brought to the gin on Saturday and the proceeds from its sale were used to maintain the livelihood of the family. Saturday was considered an outing day for most families in the community. They would arrive in town before the movie started at 1:00 PM. There was only one movie theatre in town, and attending was an important event for the children and most of the adults. The movie theatre was of course segregated. White people sat downstairs in the main area of the theatre and Black people went upstairs to a small balcony. Black people weren't able to buy the treats that were available to the White patrons because we were not allowed in the main lobby of the theatre.

To me as a child, this was Jim Crow at its worst.

Fortunately, there was one store in Giddings where all of the Black, and a few of the White, farmers would meet on Saturday. This was the only store in Giddings where African-American family could go and sit for hours, relaxing and talking to friends and neighbors. The store had all the supplies that everyone needed. The owner had built benches on the inside for Black and White men, women and children to sit. This was the only integrated place in town. The customers really seemed to enjoy this minimal accommodation. The children, Black and White, were allowed to run and play in certain areas of the store.

During the 1940s in my community of Post Oak there were no televisions or computers. However, some families were fortunate enough to have a battery radio. There was one telephone in the entire community, and it was located three miles from my home at Mr. Turner's store, across the road from the Post Oak Community School I attended until I was eleven years old and in the fifth grade.

I started school when I was five years old. My father continued to farm and my mother started working in the cafeteria at the Post Oak Community School. She would take me to school with her because during this time there were no day care facilities. I would sit in the school's cafeteria while she worked.

This went on for several days, until the first-to-third grade teacher saw me sitting there. The teacher, whom I'll never forget, was Mrs. Coleman. She lived next door to the school. She asked my mother if I could come to her class, and my mother agreed that it was a great idea. For several days my mother took me to school with her, but I wanted to ride on the big yellow school bus that passed my house on school days. Although I was the only child in my family, down the road approximately a quarter of a mile I had an uncle and aunt who had many children. My mother allowed me to ride the bus and I was very happy. I lived closer to the school than my cousins, so the school bus would pass my house and go farther down the road and pick up all of my cousins. When it returned it was almost completely filled. As I entered the bus, all of my cousins, in unison, would greet me with a big "Good Morning Curtis!" This made me feel secure and loved. My teen-aged cousin, Evelyn, would always save me a seat next to her, which I thought was wonderful.

Mrs. Coleman had a class of approximately twenty students. During class, I sat in the front row close to her. I learned my alphabet and was able to count my numbers considerably well. At the end of the school year my academic skills were comparable to the other first graders and I was promoted to the second grade. I was elated!

We were given discarded books that White students had read in their schools and had become damaged. Some had no covers, many pages had been written on or torn, and some pages were even missing. In these books, the only African-Americans mentioned were Frederick Douglas, Booker T. Washington, George Washington Carver, Phillis Wheatley (an African-American poet during the Revolutionary War) and a few others who had made positive contributions to America. However, there was no mention in our lessons of the 12 million men, women and children from the African homeland who changed forever the face and character of our world over three-and-one-half centuries.

In Mrs. Coleman's class there was no specific curriculum. All of the books were put on a table in front of the classroom and we would select the ones we could read easily. Mrs. Coleman would call each student to her desk at a given time and listen to them read. Depending on their reading skills, she would determine what level of book to use.

Quite often the third-grade students would read to the second graders, and the second-grade students would read to the first graders. This method, called "reading-learning," was practiced in all of the classrooms.

During the first hour of class, Mrs. Coleman would teach basic English to all three grades, while writing and explaining the lesson on the blackboard. Along with the English lesson, she talked to us about respect for each other; to be reliant and resourceful persons.

The school had no gas or electric heating. The classrooms had a large wood burning stove, located on the left side, a few feet from the back door. There also was an area for wood to be stored. Thirty minutes before school was out, the entire class had chores to perform. Some students were assigned to erase the blackboard, tidy up the classroom, while three or four students, boys and girls, were assigned to go outside to the wood pile and gather wood for the following day. Each student had a turn to perform each of these chores. This was an exciting time for us. We really looked forward to our turn because we were able to get out of the classroom and do something we enjoyed. When we arrived at school the next morning the teacher or the janitor would have loaded the stove, and the classroom was always warm and comfortable.

In the early 1940s, my father continued to farm, but he was seldom able to make a profit from the crops he produced. Quite often the weather was unfavorable for the growth of a specific product. Many times when the crop's yield was adequate, he was unable to get enough workers to harvest and take it to the market. Consequently, he had to get bank loans almost yearly to continue to farm, hoping that each coming year would be better than the last; however, it never was. Over a period of years the entire fifty acres was lost to the banks through liens.

Chapter 3

Education of the Estes Family

The first person to have a formal education in my family, beyond elementary and high school, was my cousin George Kerr, a relative on the Estes side of the family. He attended Paul Quinn College in Waco, Texas in the early 1900s, the oldest Historically Black College in Texas, founded in 1872. It is an important part of the city's history, known as the "Athens of the Brazos." Paul Quinn College is now in Dallas. Cousin George majored in elementary and secondary education and taught in many schools throughout the state of Texas.

In the 1930s, my mother Ella and her sister Amanda were the first of the Jones family to go to college. Both graduated from Prairie View A&M College, another of the Historically Black Colleges. My mother taught school for several years and my Aunt Amanda taught for thirty-five years. It became a tradition in my family that the females would go to college while the males stayed home and worked the farm. My mother had three brothers and my father had five, but none of them attended college. Most of the males, when reaching the age of eighteen, would join the military and remain for twenty or thirty years.

This tradition continued through the next generation. My sister Edna and most of our female relatives were able to go to college. In the late 1940s, Edna attended Huston Tillotson College (now University), an Historically Black College in Austin founded in 1875, where she received a bachelor's degree in education. The school's website states that HTU awards bachelor's degrees in business, education, humanities, natural science, social science, science and technology. Edna then enrolled at the University of Texas in Austin in 1955. The next year she received a master's degree, being one of the first Black students to attend and receive a degree from the university.

In 1951, at the age of seventeen, I entered Prairie View A&M University, majoring in agricultural economics, with a minor in rural sociology, receiving a BS degree in 1955.

Most of my family who attended college went

to Historically Black Colleges and Universities. This was because we lived in the Jim Crow South and the state of Texas, where schools barred their doors to Black Americans. It wasn't until 1950 that the U.S. Supreme Court ruled, in *Sweatt v. Painter*, that Black law students could attend the University of Texas Law School, and only in 1962 was Dana Jean Smith, an 18-year-old Black woman, able to attend Southwest Texas State College, now Texas State University, after a federal court order.

Chapter 4

The Move to Houston

When I was ten, in 1944, my parents divorced. My mother and I moved to Houston, Texas, which was approximately 120 miles south of Post Oak. My mother had some health issues that had to be attended to, so she decided that for this period of time it would be best that I lived with my aunt Amanda and her daughter, Geraldine, in Galveston. While in Galveston, I attended George Washington Elementary School for one year in the fifth grade. My aunt also was my teacher. Initially this was quite unpleasant, but I was able to adjust.

After the school year, I rejoined my mother in Houston. For almost three years, we lived with my uncle Odell and his wife Vera on Elgin Street in the third ward area. In 1945, Black people lived in separate areas of town called "wards." But Black people were self-sufficient and productive. They owned businesses, including theaters, restaurants, insurance companies, funeral homes and banks.

While living on Elgin Street I met Oscar Rogers and we became best friends. We both were the only children in our family so our bond was like brothers. We walked to school together, rode bikes together, and pretty much did everything together. We watched each other's backs. We remain friends today.

This was during World War II when most American servicemen were deployed in different parts of the world. Due to the lack of manpower in the United States, there were many jobs available for women. My mother was able to secure a job with the Brown Shipyard, a ship building company that had a contract with the U.S. government. She had gone to school to become a welder, but during the 1940s in the South, because of Jim Crow laws, they would not hire a Black woman as a welder, so she was hired as a janitor. The job required her to sweep and clean the deck of the ships which were laden with asbestos material. She worked for the shipyard company until the end of World War II in 1945.

That year I graduated from Blackshear Elementary, a kindergarten through sixth-grade school. After that I attended Jack Yates High School in the third ward area and finished in June of 1951, at the age of seventeen.

After employment with the Brown Shipyard Company, my mother started working at Herman Hospital in the Houston Medical Center. She became a Licensed Vocational Nurse, assigned to the recovery room of the surgery department. She worked in this capacity for thirty-five years and retired in 1980.

When I was fifteen, my mother bought a house on Clay Street, in the third-ward area, for $2,500. These tract houses extended north and south for three blocks. Most were painted white, with a variety of trim colors. Some had beautiful green lawns, although they were rather small, with colorful climbing roses cascading over the front-yard fences and gates. At the end of the three blocks going north was the Temple Lumber Yard, where the sounds of electric saws and other loud noises were always present. My mother and I lived in the middle of the block near the lumber yard. Five days a week, during the day, it was always noisy. We were really happy that the company did not have a night shift. At the end of the three blocks going South was a railroad track. My friends and I knew the schedule of each train, and became accustomed to the sounds of the whistles and the rattle of the train coaches.

There weren't many children in my

neighborhood. We played and shared the little we had with each other. We were always respectful to the adults. The adults knew all of the children by name, and any parent or adult could discipline any child.

There was one high school for Black children in the third-ward community, which was located near my uncle's home from where we had just moved. After our move to Clay Street, I would ride the public bus in the morning. After school, I would either ride the bus or walk home with several of my friends who lived in the same neighborhood. It was fun walking home during the summer months, but during the fall and winter months it rained and could be extremely cold, so we would ride the bus most of the time.

I would often ride the bus from downtown Houston at Roberts and Leland. When it stopped on the corner near my house to let Black passengers off, the White passengers would comment on the dilapidated houses, making statements such as "what a dump!" I was embarrassed to get off at that stop, so I would ride to the next stop where the houses were more attractive and in fairly good repair.

My sons and I went to Houston for our family reunion in 2010. I wanted to show them where I lived during those eight years. Unfortunately, the entire three blocks of tract houses had been torn down and there were only vacant lots. Around the corner, one block away, there were beautiful townhouses that had been recently built. I didn't realize when growing up that we were only about two miles south of downtown Houston. Now this neighborhood has become part of the inner city.

As a teenager I was involved in basketball and baseball. I didn't play for the high school but played for the little league in my ward. We were called the "Junior Pros." Our coach was a highly respected young man who worked every day but dedicated his time to coaching children. His name was William Lowe. We practiced after school daily at Emancipation Park, which was huge, covering an entire block on Dowling Street, the main street in the third ward area, which had clubs, taxi cab stations, pool halls, restaurants, a bakery and all types of stores. But most impressive was the Eldorado Ballroom. This is where Black entertainers from all over the United States would come to entertain.

On Friday evenings, after practice, my friend, Harold Hopkins, and I would often sit and watch the entertainers and the people who attended the ballroom. All who attended, both men and women, were beautifully dressed. The men wore handsome tailored suits and the women wore expensive stylish dresses. Harold and I were deeply impressed and decided that we would like to go and see the entertainers perform. We agreed that when school was out for the summer we would get a job and earn enough money to buy the appropriate clothes to wear to the ballroom.

That summer of 1951 we both found jobs. I was able to get a job as an orderly in Herman Hospital, where my mother worked in the same department. The hospital was an old building with a new building attached. The new building was for White patients, and the old building was for what they called "the colored." This was Jim Crow at its worst, an example of how the theory of "separate but equal" doesn't really exist. The entrances to the hospital were separate as were all of the facilities, including the cafeteria and restrooms.

The surgery department was located in the new building on the third floor. When a Black patient was scheduled for surgery, I would have to take the elevator in the new building to the basement and travel through a tunnel approximately one block long to the old building. From there, I took another elevator up to the floor where the patient was located, then returned the patient to the new building for surgery. As an orderly, I would make several trips during my shift. I worked at the hospital for the entire four years I was in college.

By the end of summer, Harold and I both had saved enough money to get the outfits that we needed to go to the Eldorado Ballroom. I was able to purchase a nice Black suit, hat, shoes, shirt and all of the necessary accessories. Harold bought a dark blue suit. We decided that we would get dressed and try getting into the ballroom. We were both seventeen years old and a little over six feet tall. We knew that the only prerequisite for getting in was to be dressed properly, be respectful to others, and not to talk too loudly. One Friday night we approached the pay window, paid our five dollars, and we were admitted. We were very proud of our achievement. After that night, we went to the ballroom whenever we liked. This was really an exciting time for us. One of the entertainers, Johnny "Guitar" Watson, grew up one block from the school and went to Jack Yates High School with Harold and me. Some of the other entertainers who frequented the ballroom were Big Joe Turner, B.B. King, Ike and Tina Turner, and Little Richard.

I graduated high school in June of 1951. I had

no idea what I would do for the future. In August my mother told me that I was going to Prairie View A&M College, which was located fifty miles from Houston, and I was to major in agriculture. She had applied to college for me and didn't tell me until I was accepted, so it came as a big shock. She felt that this would be the ideal field for me because she had grown up on the farm and also had gone to Prairie View A&M in the 1930s. She was familiar with the agriculture teachers and county agents. Fortunately, a couple of my friends were also going. One of them had a truck, so we packed up my big old trunk, threw it on the truck, and I was off. Texas A&M was the same distance from my home as Prairie View A&M, but I couldn't go there as this was before *Brown v. Board of Education.*

I entered Prairie View A&M in September of 1951, and finished in June of 1955, with a major in agricultural economics and a minor in rural sociology. In my Junior year I met Theresa Burrell, and after several years of courtship we were married. In 1955, we both found employment as school teachers. Theresa was hired as a high-school English teacher in Jefferson, Texas, located in the eastern part of the state, and I was hired as an elementary teacher in a small town in the western part of Texas, called Spur. Our jobs were approximately five-hundred miles apart.

On May 17, 1954, the United States Supreme Court, in *Brown v. Board of Education,* declared that state laws establishing separate public schools for Black and White students to be unconstitutional and a violation of the fourteenth amendment. The principal behind school segregation was, of course, "separate but equal" accommodations for the races. But in 1955 the schools in Spur, Texas, were still segregated as were all of the schools in the state. Black students still attended schools with substandard facilities, out-of-date textbooks and often no basic school supplies. In 1964, a full decade after *Brown v. Board of Education,* more than 98% of Black children in the South still attended segregated schools. There was intensified resistance in the South, particularly among White supremacist groups and government officials sympathetic to the segregationist cause. U.S. Senator Harry F. Byrd, Sr. of Virginia started the Massive Resistance Movement in the 1960s that sought to pass laws to keep public schools from being desegregated.

I taught in a three-classroom school with grades K through twelve with three other teachers. My cousin, George Kerr, who at the time was seventy-five years old, was the principal and also the teacher of grades nine through twelve. Cousin Louise, his wife, taught grades one through three. I taught grades four through eight and had about twenty-five students, six to seven in each grade level. The school had no library, gymnasium or cafeteria. But the schools across town where White students attended had all of these amenities. Clearly they were "separate" but not "equal."

I was also the school's bus-driver and the basketball coach for boys and girls. During basketball season, the team was invited to participate in a tournament on a Saturday at a school nearby, which involved girls and boys. All of the players were eager and excited to participate. I drove the bus and several parents accompanied me as chaperons. When we arrived at the school, it was decided that the boy's teams would play first, and our team won. It would be several hours before we were to play again. The parents and I decided that this would be a good time for our team to take a lunch break. The students were allowed to go by themselves to a restaurant several blocks away. On their return the parents and I realized that they had had a little more than just lunch. After questioning they did finally admit that they drank some beer. They tried to play the game but their basketball skills were greatly impaired, and of course we lost the tournament.

The following day, my cousin George, the principle, asked me, "How was the tournament?" My reply was, "We did quite well during the morning games, but didn't do well in the afternoon." I never told him what really happened. This was our first and last tournament. Our small community in Spur, Texas, being smaller than many others communities, had excellent rapport between parents, teachers and students.

Chapter 5

Military Service

In 1957, after a year of teaching, I entered the army. Following several months of basic training, I was deployed to Okinawa, Japan, a part of the Is-lands surrounded by the Pacific Ocean and the Sea of Japan. The "Battle of Okinawa" was the last major battle of World War II, and one of the bloodiest. After devastating casualties on both sides, Japan surrendered to American-led allies on September 2, 1945.

Okinawa is made up of four mountainous islands and hundreds of smaller islets. They form a huge arc in the Pacific off the eastern coast of the Asian mainland. The Japanese are tough, inventive, and hard-working. These qualities lifted their nation from ruin after World War II to become one of the leading industrial countries of the world. When I arrived in Okinawa in 1957, twelve years after the end of the war, I was assigned to the Armed Services Police Company as the company's clerk, a specialist fourth class. During this period, the Okinawans had no police department, governor or government officials. The island was under martial law and the American military police force was responsible for enforcing the law and keeping the peace. My tour of duty in Okinawa ended in July, 1959.

In August I returned to my mother's home in Houston. I had finished my two years of active duty and now it was time to fulfill my reserve obligation of six years. I reported to the nearest reserve center, which was located near my mother's home. My M.O.S. (master occupation specialty) was clerk or administrative assistant as this is what the military had trained me for. When I arrived at the reserve center in Houston, to my surprise, it was a huge office with ten to twenty reservists. I glanced quickly over the group and I didn't see any Black reservists, male or female. I thought that this was rather strange and unusual, but this was Houston, where Jim Crow still existed. According to my M.O.S., I should have been assigned to that office. But even in the military services in Houston at that time segregation was prevalent.

After reporting to the officer in charge and showing him my release papers, he stated that he would notify me soon regarding my assignment.

Two weeks later, I received my discharge papers stating that no reserve obligation was needed. After two years of duty in Okinawa, Japan, defending America's policy, I was still considered a second-class citizen.

Chapter 6

Wiley College

After my discharge from the army in 1959, I enrolled in the Department of Education at Wiley College in Marshall, Texas so I could get my teaching certificate. Wiley College, an HBCU, boasts of being the oldest Historically Black College west of the Mississippi River. This school was also the focus of the movie "The Great Debaters," starring Denzel Washington. It was founded in 1873, during a time of extreme tension between Black and White populations.

Marshall is in Eastern Texas, the worst part of the state during Jim Crow. There were lots of places we couldn't go. Even in my uniform, I couldn't sit down in public restaurants and eat as other Americans could. And we couldn't try on any clothes: "If you try them, you buy them."

And so in 1960, I was one of those students sitting in at the lunch counters in various restaurants in Marshall. Although we were jailed and ridiculed many times, we never relinquished our desire to be served and to eat in public places as other citizens could. The Chancellor of the college would come bail us out; he'd ask how we were and tell us what a beautiful job we were doing. This was a man with a Ph.D. The police at the jail, while some didn't have more than a fourth or fifth grade education, called him "boy" and other derogatory names.

As we were sitting in, we knew we were standing up for the best of the American dream. We believed we were guiding the nation back to those great wells of democracy which were dug by the founding fathers as they wrote the Declaration of Independence and the Constitution of the United States. During my two years at Wiley College I fought for justice and equality for all people who were discriminated against. And today I continue to do so.

I reflect back to Dr. King's speech, "The American Dream," that was given to the graduating class at Lincoln University in Pennsylvania on June 6, 1961, where he stated:

Slavery and segregation have been strange paradoxes in a nation founded on the principal that all men are created equal. This is what the Swedish sociologist, Gunner Myrdal, referred to as the American dilemma. But the shape of the world today does not permit us the luxury of an anemic democracy. The price that America must pay for the continued oppression of the Negro and other minority groups is the price of its own destruction. If America is to remain a first-class nation, it can no longer have second-class citizens. Now, more than ever before, America is challenged to bring its noble dream into reality, and those who are working to implement the American dream are the true saviors of democracy.

While attending classes in the morning, I was employed at the Marshall Hotel Restaurant as a dishwasher. I worked six hours a day, five days a week. There was a ballroom located on the fourth floor of the hotel that was open Friday and Saturday nights, and I soon became a waiter there as well. Two nights a week, after finishing my dishwashing job, I would hurry to the locker room and change from my apron to black slacks, shined black shoes, white shirt, bow tie, white jacket, and a new burst of energy.

Of course the ballroom was segregated, with all White patrons and all Black employees. For my first few weeks as a waiter, I was called "boy" and many other names that I prefer not to repeat. Eventually they did realize I have a name. As a dishwasher, I was paid $45 a week, but as a waiter, my tips per night were $30 to $40, plus salary. You could say my income was adequate for this period of time and was a tremendous help in paying my way through school.

In 1961, I received a B.A. in Elementary Education and a teacher's certificate from Wiley. Then in 1962, after completing all of the required courses to get a teacher's certificate, I started looking for employment as an elementary teacher in the immediate community.

For at least nine months I searched for a job without success. Because I had an uncle in San Francisco who had gone there during World War II, I decided to write and ask him about potential employment in that city. He stated that he was a good friend of the supervisor of the medical records department at Kaiser Hospital where he worked as a maintenance man and would ask her regarding my employment. Several days later he called and told me that a file clerk's job would be available in a month, and if I wanted it, it was mine.

Chapter 7

San Francisco

I arrived in San Francisco on September 17, 1963, and started work at Kaiser Hospital one month before President Kennedy was assassinated in Dallas by Lee Harvey Oswald. This was a tremendous shock to me and the entire nation.

While working at Kaiser Hospital I shared a two-bedroom apartment with my aunt Mag. The apartment was owned by my aunt Amanda, who lived in the upstairs apartment. She was the aunt I had lived with when I was eleven years old in Galveston when she was also my teacher. Eighteen years later she was still teaching school.

In June of 1964, after my wife had completed the school year in Jefferson, Texas, where she had taught high school English for seven years, she moved to San Francisco to join me. While reading the want ads in the local newspaper she saw an article by an agency stating that teachers were needed in Merced, California. My wife and I went to Merced and directly to the District

Personnel Office. After speaking to the personnel direc-
tor and showing her the necessary credentials, we were
both hired on the spot for the forthcoming September.

My wife was assigned the position of librarian in
one of the junior high schools, and I was assigned to
teach a fifth-grade class in one of the elementary schools.
During our first year in Merced, my wife and I met a
co-worker, Larry Finlayson, who was a foster parent of
several African-American boys. He would often ask my
wife and I if we could assist him in determining the appropriate care and rearing of these boys. We didn't have
any children or parental experience. However, we did
make a commitment to become co-parents, and through
this relationship, we became close friends.

The next year, Larry was hired as a sixth grade teacher
at Lincoln Elementary School in Berkeley, California,
where the University of California (UCB) is located.
Berkeley is a rather small city of about 120,000 residents,
but there are about 40,000 students attending UCB.
Lincoln Elementary School is located in South Berkeley,
an area where predominantly African-Americans and a
few Asian-Americans live. The school's population was
similar. Some of the teachers had little or no experience
in teaching in an integrated setting.

Mr. Wells, the principal of Lincoln, knew that in
the next few years, when busing began, there would

be an influx of students from every part of the city and he would need teachers who had the experience and training to work with children of every ethnicity and background. Mr. Wells asked Larry if he had an administrative credential, and he did. He accepted the job as vice-principal and was given the assignment of recruiting teachers who had experience teaching in an integrated setting. Larry recommended my wife and me. We were hired immediately.

Chapter 8
Berkeley Unified School District

In September of 1966, my wife and I started working at the Berkeley Unified School District. My wife was hired as a librarian at the West Campus, and I was assigned to Lincoln Elementary School in South Berkeley as a six-grade teacher. At that time there seemed to be an abundance of school supplies, equipment and special activities in areas such as music, art, physical education and teacher aides. I had two aides assigned to my classroom and they were extremely helpful working with small groups and one-on-one teaching.

One of my students, whom I will call Billy, was mischievous, constantly walking, talking and meddling with his classmates. He often needed to go to the restroom or to see the nurse. I called Billy's mother and told her about Billy's behavior and the frequent visits to the restroom and the nurse's office. She was shocked by the news, and stated that Billy didn't have any medical problems, and his behavior in the classroom was unwarranted. She asked if she could come to the classroom and observe his behavior. My classroom had two doors with small windows near the top. One morning, while I was standing in front of the classroom, I noticed Billy's mother looking through the rear door's window. Billy was up, out of his seat, moving around in the classroom as usual. Suddenly Billy's mother burst through the door and started spanking him. I was shocked, and the students were too. Eventually I was able to calm Billy's mother down and get them both out of the classroom. After that, I would report discipline problems to the principle, assistant principal, or counselor, but seldom directly to the parent.

My second year at Lincoln, prior to the opening of school, I was instrumental in helping to set up an in-service workshop for two weeks. The purpose was to familiarize teacher aides with the available instructional materials, how they could be used most effectively in the classroom, and how to help children develop their self-confidence and ability to relate to others. While the children were in small groups, I observed that they were relaxed, attentive, and seemed to learn more effectively from their peers than the teacher. From this observation, my teacher aide and I set up groups within the classroom. The students who possessed most of the academic skills were made the team leaders. The function of the team leader was to make sure that each member of the group made a positive contribution, either written or verbally.

This method of teaching proved to be a success. At the end of the school year students were given the usual proficiency tests and they all had made tremendous improvement. Seventy-five percent of the students were on grade level. The following school year a great number of the teachers in the school used this technique.

In 1968, the Berkeley Unified School District became the first major school system to voluntarily integrate its schools. The city of Berkeley is a community rich in diversity. This can be seen in the various racial, ethic, economic, educational, and linguistic backgrounds of the population that inhabits the city.

The district initially implemented a school desegregation system by using "paired schools," and instituted a mandatory "two-way busing system." Under this plan, the district transported students from the predominately non-White West Berkeley to the predominately White East Berkeley for kindergarten to third grade, and East Berkeley students to West Berkeley for fourth to sixth grades, thus eliminating school segregation created by the de-facto residential segregation within the city.

Following the commitment to further desegregate the junior high schools, the district created two schools that served students in grades seven and eight. Junior high school boundaries were drawn in a manner that would ensure racial integration in the two schools that cut across city boundaries. The Berkeley Unified School District believed that diversity in the student population enriches the educational experiences of students and encourages positive relationships across racial and economic lines by breaking the cycle of racial hostility.

Contrary to what the BUSD believed and hoped would happen by busing students from one area of the city to another, the positive effect did not happen immediately. While most of the classrooms were integrated, many of the students were still segregated socially. I noticed that on the playground, during recess, the girls were separated by race. But the boys who were playing sports were fairly integrated, and they seemed to play and communicate quite well.

The problem was that some students did not receive the education they deserved. At Lincoln, which was renamed Malcolm X, most of the classrooms were racially mixed. However, in these classes were students who were performing on a level below their grade. There were students assigned to the sixth grade who were performing academically on a fourth- or fifth-grade level.

At this time there also was a decline in teacher aides and other supportive services. This caused students who were below grade level to become somewhat neglected. Most of these students were African-American or spoke English as a second language. These students were getting farther behind academically because of the lack of one-on-one attention. A great number started acting out in the classroom, creating a discipline problem. Several junior high school teachers told me when these students reached junior high, they were placed in low achieving classrooms. These classrooms were called "track classes." They did not prepare students as well as the other classrooms did.

Before busing began, there were many African-American male teachers at Malcolm X. After busing, I was dismayed at the dwindling number of African-American men in classroom positions and in administrative positions. One reason could have been that teachers were not paid very well. To support a family on a teacher's salary was almost impossible. Many of the African-American male teachers had found employment in other industries. Thus they were not encouraged to remain in the school system, especially in the lower grade levels.

I felt that the school district did did not provide a system that is sensitive to, and supportive of, children and teachers. I also felt that upper administration had lost touch with the needs of African-American children and other minorities.

Eventually I decided to enroll in the counseling department at San Francisco State University. My hope was to get a job as counselor in the Berkeley school system and to work with some of these students in need. I started the program in 1972 and received a master's degree in Counseling and Guidance two years later. I applied for a counseling position several times and had interviews but no success in securing a job. There were many counseling jobs available in the district in the 1970s, but they often were given to "special individuals" who had less than a counseling degree. I believed that the system was seriously unfair. I felt that the political infighting and the jockeying for certain positions in the school district was not conducive to producing good teachers, administrators or counselors. I remained as a teacher at Malcolm X until 1976 when I left to teach at several other schools in Berkeley.

I always enjoyed teaching and took great pride in my work with children. But after twenty years of teaching, in April of 1981, I became ill with Bell's Palsy. This is a condition that causes a temporary weakness or paralysis of the muscles in the face. It can occur when the nerves that controls your facial muscles becomes inflamed, swollen, or compressed. Although teaching eighteen years in Berkeley was enjoyable, it was also stressful because of administrative and economic pressures. Budget cuts resulted in eliminating music, art, and physical education.

At first, I took medical leave from teaching. During my recovery, I worked with my wife who owned a landscape design business in the Berkeley area. Quite often I would go to work with her and assist in whatever needed to be done. I was not very good at reading the blueprints she had drawn, so she would designate the area where the plants and flowers were to be planted and I would dig the holes.

Gardening was both physically stimulating and therapeutic for me. At the age of forty-eight, this was the first time I had an opportunity to do physical work. I found it relaxing and serene working outdoors with the plants and flowers and being able to set my own hours, to be in the open and fresh air, and to see the fruits of my labor.

The Littles were among my wife's customers who lived in Berkeley. One day, as my wife and I were working at their place, Mrs. Little asked me if I had a lawnmower and if I was interested in mowing the lawn. The answer was yes. She was my first customer as a gardener.

The name of our landscaping and gardening business was "Growing Needs." We owned one truck, which had a beautiful logo designed by my wife. I would always park the truck in an area where the logo was visible for drivers, passengers, and pedestrians. We started advertising in several newspapers and in the summer months we had at least ten additional customers. I was scheduled to start teaching again in September of 1982, but in August, at the age of forty-eight, I resigned my position with the Berkeley Unified School District.

For the next two years I employed several different workers in my gardening business, but most of them decided that the work was too physical, or they found other employment that they preferred. During the summer of 1984, a friend who taught school in Oakland worked with me for two months of his vacation. I had one employee at that time.

My friend told me that when I would leave the job site to go some other place to do an estimate, the employee would stop working and constantly complained of how hard the work was. The work was strenuous at times, but not impossible. Most of the jobs I had were overgrown gardens with tall weeds, plus small trees and vines that had to be removed. My friend lived in Oakland and in his neighborhood were many men from Cambodia who were unable to find employment because of a lack of language skills. He said they were skilled in many types of work and were willing and eager to work.

The following day, I asked him to bring me one man. He brought me a 28-year-old named Paul. Paul had very little gardening experience but had many other skills. He was a skilled mechanic, brick layer, and knew how to operate heavy equipment. He was willing to work hard. On sunny days, Paul and I worked from 9:00 A.M. to dark, usually nine to ten hours daily. After a year, with my wife doing the design work, and with Paul and I doing the maintenance, we had more customers than the three of us could service. I asked Paul to bring me another man. Then there were three of us doing maintenance work and cleanup jobs, working eight hours daily, five days a week.

With the addition of the third employee I was able to spend more time in my office, which was a room in my home at Yolo Avenue in Berkeley. This was the early 1980s; I didn't have a computer and most of my records were kept on columnar pads. But for me it was quite adequate.

Paul had been my employee the longest, he knew the daily routine, the time each customer was to be serviced. He was the designated driver, auto mechanic, tool repairman, and the foreman. The business continued to run smoothly for many years.

In 1986, my high school in Houston was having its thirty-fourth class reunion, and I decided to attend. I went to the reunion with the intention of only spending three days but ended up spending almost three months because my mother was hospitalized with a prognosis of terminal cancer. After three months my mother passed away. She was 77 years old.

I am an only child, so after my mother's death I had the responsibilities of paying all of her bills and the sale of the family home. But while in Houston, I was able to keep my business going with the help of my foreman Paul and my wife.

When I returned to Berkeley in July of 1986, my wife and I decided to separate, and a few months later we were divorced. My oldest son Curtis was twelve years old and his brother Jonathan was nine. I was still recovering from my mother's death. Separation from my wife and the new responsibility of being a single parent were somewhat overwhelming. As custodian of my sons, our perceptions, life styles, and goals in life took a 180 degree turn. After a few months I was able to adjust to the new situation, but for my sons, the absence of their mother presented many issues. For several years after the divorce both of my sons expressed disbelief, anxiety and depression. I encouraged them to fill the void with after-school sports, which did not do much academically, but did redirect their attention to becoming proficient athletes and eventually the capable individuals they are today.

From 1986, until many years later, I had custody of my sons, and was the sole owner of the landscaping business. With the inheritance from my mother, I paid my wife the portion of the equity that was due her and also became the sole owner of the property on Yolo Avenue. I continued the landscaping business for several more years, but decided, after thirty-two years of working, that it was time for me to retire in 2006 at the age of seventy-two.

Chapter 9

Amistad House

I had lived in two different affordable housing communities for seniors, and in 2002, after being on the waiting list for five years, I was able to move into an apartment at the Amistad House in Berkeley, run by Satellite Affordable Housing Association (SAHA).

Amistad House is an incredible community. Its central location allows me to go for daily walks and do my own shopping. There is immediate access to public transportation. Also, the North Berkeley Senior Center is located only three blocks from my apartment.

The Senior Center has many activities and serves hot nutritious meals five days a week. It is dedicated to promoting a dignified, healthy quality of life for older adults that include vital services, opportunities to develop meaningful fellowship, lifelong learning activities, meeting rooms and a Wheels on Meals program.

After retiring from my landscaping business in 2006, I started going to the center for lunch almost daily. After attending for several months, I became a member of the Advisory Council. The Advisory Council assists and advises participants, volunteers, and staff on activities, schedules, services, projects, policies, and programs. In addition, the council sponsors activities involving center participants, advocates for senior citizen needs and concerns, and develops guidelines and recommendations for procedures at the center.

There are a variety of enrichment activities and support services offered at the center designed to empower seniors in the community, including how to discover new ways to be actively engaged in living. Some of the activities are arts and crafts, computers, exercise and dance, foreign language and music. There is a sports room located on the first floor where a pool table is located. I noticed that the seniors who were involved in the game really enjoy themselves. I had played pool and enjoyed it when in the army. I decided I would like to try to play the game again. The seniors who were playing, both women and men, were very good. I knew it would take a while before I would become competitive with the others, but I was determined to become better, and over a period of approximately six months I became proficient.

Today, at the age of eighty-seven, I still enjoy playing pool. The game, if played properly, is a challenge. It requires concentration, focus, eye and hand coordination and, most of all, skill and resolve. Most pool players have played for years. There is no age or gender limit. The desire to play and enjoy the game is the only prerequisite. The game of pool leads to improved physical balance and increased sociability, which are essential to continue leading a healthy life.

Chapter 10

The Next Generation

The following is an account by my oldest son, Curtis, of the time we lived in Berkeley and his life since then. It includes his perspective on our lifestyle, having a single parent, and his eventual involvement in the real estate industry.

When I left the home I lived in for fifteen years in North Berkeley in 1990, at the age of eighteen, I felt that my life would be in disarray for years to come. My dad and I had been struggling financially for a long time.

During high school my brother and I worked and participated in our school's sports program as football and rugby players. As a high school senior I worked for a poultry store, and received credits that were transferred to school units. This gave me enough credits to graduate high school in 1991.

Education was not my priority in high school. I became lost amidst the almost three thousand students who attended Berkeley High. I honestly do not remember writing a paper in high school. After high school I worked in part time jobs and attempted to take classes at junior college, but the need to make money took precedence. I tried to go to school and work at the same time, but lacked the academic skills that would have allowed me to multi-task with greater success.

My father had given my mother a large part of his inheritance when they divorced. Then he was involved in a bitter property dispute with neighbors for years. The neighbors became hostile upon learning that my father wanted to build a detached home on our large property for the three of us and turn the main house into a nursing home for seniors.

My father has always fought for what he believed in. But he was continuously confronted with one opposing petition and court battle after another. Although he made multiple changes to the plans, it was never good enough. Eventually, he was able to complete a one-bedroom cottage. But when it was all done, he had spent thousands of dollars for lawyers and construction expenses. He could not bounce back, and in 1991, the house was sold in a short sale.

When I moved out I found a job as a flatbed truck-loader with United Parcel Service while my father and younger brother moved to a two-bedroom apartment in El Cerrito. This was when I became interested in real estate and realized I would work in that industry.

During that time I watched my father, an incredibly strong man, hit his mental and financial bottom. I believe what kept him going was love for his two sons and the transition into affordable housing. After losing our home in the stressful manner we did, it took years for him to recover.

My father's first stop in affordable housing was the San Pablo Senior Center in Oakland, where he lived for two and a half years, and then two and a half years at the Oakland Center Towers. After that he settled in at the Amistad House, which for the last twenty years has been an incredible and supportive community for him. His apartment is one of the cleanest and most organized I have seen, which is something I believe his mother, and eventually the military service, instilled in him. SAHA (Satellite Affordable Housing Associates) makes sure the building and his apartment meet and exceed the living standards required by law.

Amistad House will be my father's final home, a place he has found complete inner peace and happiness. I go to see him every week, and at 87 years old, his face has never been brighter. I give him updates on my progress, and although it is hard for me to get a word in due to his excitement, he slows down when I talk about my plans because he knows what I have been through.

My father gave my brother and I an incredible work ethic and determination. In our household there were many tasks to be done, from house cleaning, to yard work. These chores were designed to prepare us to become resourceful and independent.

In 2005, I decided to obtain my real estate license. I began working for Prudential Realty in Berkeley. I quickly went from knowing very little about real estate to being one of the most productive salesmen in my office. In 2007, I was one of the top ten producing agents, but despite my success, as the economy and housing market crumbled in 2008, so did my real estate sales business. I decided to return to school, this time with the support of my wife.

During the 2011 school year, I came across a recruiting table for Chase Bank, looking to hire a personal banker for one of their retail branches. I put my name on a list of interested students, and within a day I had passed an assessment and was given an opportunity to interview in front of a panel of branch managers. Eventually I received the job and began three years of working for Chase. During this period, I left school again, thinking that I had found a place where I would be happy, but many changes happened in the mortgage industry and I found myself looking in another direction.

In 2013, my wife and I came across a real estate unit

in East Oakland on 75th Avenue. A man in his eighties came to us with a four-unit property that he was having a difficult time managing and wanted to sell. We immediately jumped at the chance to buy the property. After months of figuring out ways to get enough money to pay off personal debt and collect a down payment, we purchased the property from the owner without a real estate agent.

Purchasing the property was the best thing that ever happened to us, despite the challenges we faced the first two years. When we closed escrow, we had no money left for repairs and the property was not cash flowing. There was drug addiction, tenants not paying their rent on time, and there were no lease agreements. I decided to begin talking and building rapport with the tenants.

In 2015, my wife and I moved into an apartment in the back of the property. I returned to school to finish my undergraduate degree. This was the first time I was able to focus primarily on school. I gradually worked my way up to a full load of classes, making sure that I did as well as I could along the way. In two and a half years, I remodeled three units in our building and used the rent from the units to pay the mortgage, garbage and water for the entire property. We were left with a small amount of money to put away for emergencies.

I received my degree in Business Administration,

with options in Finance and Real Estate Management, at California State University East Bay in 2016. Academically, I have faced challenges that I believe stem from a lack of counseling and guidance in the school system at a young age.

I am most proud of the fact that we have created a healthier environment for our tenants. While going through the challenges of managing a difficult property and going to school, my wife and I decided to divorce. She allowed me to buy her out of her portion of the property. Since the buyout I have been able to remove the tenants who were not paying rent and have been able to offer the units to individuals transitioning from assisted living facilities following addiction, incarceration or homelessness. I have had multiple neighbors thank us for changing the feeling of the neighborhood. This is a passion that I plan to continue with my own real estate company.

Although there are significant issues living in East Oakland, I have never felt the sense of community I now get from my neighborhood. Everyone knows each other and they all look out for one another. My experience cleaning up and managing property has given me a sense of purpose and satisfaction. I want to work in affordable housing because I believe that the foundation to any successful transition in life, whether raising a child or living out one's last years, starts with a healthy living environment.

I loved real estate when I was selling homes as an agent, but I was not fulfilled the way I am now. There is no better feeling than being able to offer someone housing, especially when that person has been met with challenges. Where someone else may see a low income, economically challenged neighborhood, I see opportunity for others and myself, and would like to be part of finding housing solutions in urban areas where it is desperately needed. Housing is an essential component to establishing a personal foundation in life. A healthy living environment helps stabilize one's job, can create a focus on school, and helps families spend time together. In my opinion, these are essential components that help perpetuate personal growth.

Now we'll return to the conclusion of my father's story.

Chapter 11
The Persistence of Jim Crow

After a year of teaching, and before entering the military in 1957, I lived in the South and became accustomed to a society that was designed to segregate Americans of European descent from those of African, American Indian, Asian and other origins. This situation has existed since colonial days.

The term Jim Crow originally referred to a Black character in an old song, and was the name of a popular dance in the 1820s. Around 1828, a man named "Thomas Daddy Rice" developed a routine in which he blackened his face and sang and danced in imitation of an old decrepit Black man. Rice published the words to the song, "Jump, Jim Crow, Jump" in 1830.

In 1896, the United States Supreme Court ruled that Jim Crow "separate but equal" laws segregating Black and White Americans were constitutional in *Plessy v. Ferguson*. In a speech on the Senate floor on March 23, 1900, Ben Tillman of South Carolina declared, "We of the South have never recognized the right of the Negro to govern White men, and we never will. We have never believed him to be equal of the White man, and we will not submit to his gratifying his lust on our wives and daughters without lynching him." Between the years 1865 and 1950, well over 3,000 African-Americans were victims of lynching. [17] Jim Crow Laws were prevalent from the 1880s into the 1960s, and even longer in some southern states. These laws have significantly affected me, my family, and the lives of all African-Americans. These laws not only encouraged "separate but equal" treatment, but condemned Black citizens to inferior living conditions and facilities. Education was segregated as were public places such as hotels, restaurants and public transportation.

In the early 20th century, with several Black schools established, leaders such as Booker T. Washington and W.E.B. DuBois fiercely debated the future of African-American education. Washington believed vocational training was the key to stepping out of poverty and servitude; DuBois defended the enlightened views of a general education drawn from studying the arts and sciences. Today's Historically Black Colleges and

THE BITTER & THE SWEET

Universities incorporate both philosophies, providing students with technical training as well as a liberal arts education.

In our day the ugly legacy of Jim Crow laws still exists. Millions of people are currently blocked from the ballot box because of previous criminal convictions. The situation in Mississippi is notably bad. The law there has its origins in the state's notorious constitution of 1890 that was designed, in the words of the Mississippi Supreme Court, "to obstruct the exercise of the franchise by the Negro race." Today, the law denies the right to vote to one in six Black people, some 200,000 people in all.

Herman Parker Jr. is one of the people denied the right to vote in Mississippi. When he was a teenager 25 years ago he was convicted of a crime. And as he states today: "I'm a husband and father of two beautiful children, and I am proud to work for the city of Vicksburg, where I was born and raised. I am not that 19-year-old boy anymore. I am a man and deserve a voice in government because of who I am today." That is why Mr. Parker and other people in Mississippi who have long since paid their debts to society are challenging the state's discriminatory voting system. [18]

Southern politicians were so set on keeping

107

Blacks away from voting booths that they set up artificial systems to deny them the vote. Examples include reading tests with questions such as:

1. How many degrees does the hour hand of a clock turn in five minutes?
2. How many veins are there in a human body?
3. How many bubbles are there in a bar of soap?

And as I write, many states still are working to pass laws to discourage minorities from voting.

Blacks in the United States still struggle to be seen and treated as equal human beings.

James Baldwin, author, lecturer and activist, wrote, in *Sonny's Blues*:

For, while the tale of how we suffer, and how we are delighted, and how we may triumph is never new, it always must be heard. There isn't any other tale to tell, it's the only light we've got in all this darkness.

C. Van Woodward states in his book, *The Strange Career of Jim Crow*:

In Montgomery, Alabama, an ordinance compelled Black residents to take seats apart from whites on municipal buses. At the time, the 'separate but equal' standard applied, but the actual separation practiced was hardly equal. A white person never had

to stand on a Montgomery bus. In addition, it fre-
quently occurred that Blacks boarding the bus were
forced to stand in the back if all seats were taken, even
if seats were available in the white section.

On December 1, 1955, a 43-year-old Black woman named Rosa Parks refused to move to the rear of a bus in Montgomery, Alabama, so that a White male passenger could sit. Mrs. Parks possessed the courage and the resistance to refuse this ridiculous Jim Crow law. When asked later why she had refused to move to the rear of the bus, she replied, "it was a matter of dignity; I could not have faced myself, and my people, if I had moved." Throughout the South and many other areas of the country, Black people were ridiculed and plagued with similar senseless and unjust Jim Crow Laws.

Born in 1913, Mrs. Parks had been an activist for two decades before her bus stand. In 1931, she began her work alongside her husband, Raymond Parks, to overcome segregation. They were instrumental in organizing a defense for the Scottsboro Boys, nine teenagers who were falsely accused of raping two White women. The issues that animated her six decades of activism were the injustice of a criminal system that permitted wrongful accusations against Black men, disregard for Black women who had been sexually assaulted, and police brutality.

The Rosa Parks story includes the tremendous cost of her bus stand and the decades of suffering that ensued for her family. They weren't well-off. Mrs. Parks' husband worked as a barber at Maxwell Air Force Base, and Mrs. Parks spent her days in a stuffy back room at Montgomery Fair department store altering White men's suits. Five weeks after her bus stand, she lost her job; then her husband lost his. Receiving regular death threats, they never found steady work in Montgomery again. Eventually, they were forced to move to Detroit where Mrs. Parks' brother and cousin lived. In 1966, eleven years after her bus arrest, she was hired to work in U. S. Representative John Conyers's new Detroit office. But she only received an income comparable to what she and her husband had made in 1955 Alabama.

Mrs. Parks spent the next several years fighting racism in the North, "the Northern Promised Land that wasn't," as she called it, marching and organizing against housing discrimination, school segregation, employment discrimination and police brutality.

The fact that Mrs. Parks spent the second part of her life fighting the racism of the North demonstrates that racism was not a regional anachronism but a national cancer. Seeing how she placed her greatest hope in the militant spirit of young people (finding many adults "complacent") gives the lie to how commentators today use the civil rights movement to chastise Black Lives Matter for not going about change the right way.

The story of Rosa Parks reveals how false those distinctions are; how criminal justice is a key to dreams of freedom; how disruptive and persevering was the movement; and where she would be standing today. This is an essential lesson for young people and all Americans. We need to constantly be reminded to understand and grapple honestly with our country's history and envision a different road forward. [19]

Even with the persistence of the laws that were designed to deny African-Americans their civil rights, Blacks have played a vital part in the building of America's economic strength; as soldiers in all of this country's wars, as contributors to national culture, as figures of importance in sports, and as participants in the varied activities of American life.

Black History Month is about the shared experience of all African-Americans, high and low, famous and obscure, and how those experiences have shaped and challenged – and ultimately strengthened – America. Black History Month is about an unvarnished look at the past so we can create a better future. It's a reminder of where we as a country have been so that we know where we need to go.

On March 5, 2010, our 44th President, Barack Obama, signed the White House initiative on Historically Black Colleges and Universities, which included five percent or $13 million increase for the strengthening of HBCU programs and $85 million in mandatory funding for the HBCU as part of his Student Aid and Fiscal Responsibility Act.

The history of Black people in this country rests upon the graves of those who, at many times, had no choice but to sacrifice their lives for justice and freedom. As Barack Obama told students at Howard University in 2016: "To deny how far we've come would do a disservice to the cause of justice, to the legions of foot-soldiers, to our mothers, fathers, grandparents and great-grandparents who marched, toiled and suffered to make this day possible."

When future history books are written, historians will have to pause and say: "there lived a great people, a Black people, and a Black president who injected new meaning and dignity into the veins of American civilization."

As the new president said in his inauguration speech on January 20, 2009: "Let it be said by our children's children that when we were tested we refused to let this journey end, that we did not turn back nor did we falter; and with eyes fixed on the horizon and God's grace upon us, we carried forth that great gift of freedom and delivered it safely to future generations."

REFERENCES

[1]   *The Fortunes of Africa*, Martin Meredith, Page 117, Public Affairs

[2]   "America's History of Slavery Began Long Before Jamestown," Crystal Ponti, August 16, 2019, History Channel Website

[3]   "The Curious History of Anthony Johnson: From Captive African to Right-wing Talking Point," Tyler Parry, July 22, 2019, Black Perspectives Magazine.

[4   Testimony of Phil' n Bliss, *American Slavery as It is: Testimony of a Thousand Witnesses*, Theodore Dwight Weld, 1839.

[5]   "American Christianity's White-Supremacy Problem," by Michael Luo, September 2, 2020, New York Times.

[6]   "Black Colleges: Why Students Choose Them," Jacqueline Fleming, August 9, 1987, Washington Post.

[7]   *Declaration of Independence*

[8]   *Trust in Black America: Race, Discrimination, and Politics*, Shayla C. Nunnally, 2012, NYU Press.

[9]   Library of Congress Interview: *"The Murder of Emmett Till."*

[10]   "Fatal Force," Washington Post, July 21, 2021.

[11]   Harvard, T.H. Chan School of Public Health.

[12]   "Mapping the Unconscious, Racism and the Oedipal Family." Nast, Heidi J., Annals of the Association of American Geographers, Vol. 90, No. 2, Jan. 2000.

[13]   *Trauma and Self*, by Charles B. Strozier and Michael Flynn, 1996, Rowman & Littlefield, Page 20.

[14]   *The Mis-Education of the Negro*, originally published in 1933.

[15]   *The Future of Democracy*, Steve Zolno, 2016, Regent Press, Page 62.

[16]   "Black Soldiers in the U.S. Military During the Civil War," National Archives.

[17]   Smithsonian Magazine of June 18, 2020.

[18]   "Mississippi Sued Over 'Unforgiving' Voting Ban for Ex-Cons," Erik De La Garza, March 28, 2018, Courthouse News Service.

[19]   "Rosa Parks' Real Story." Jeanne Theoharis, professor of political science and the author of *The Rebellious Life of Mrs. Rosa Parks*, February 7, 2021, The New York Times.

BIBLIOGRAPHY

"Abstract of Title: A one-hundred-fifty-seven and one-half acres of land out of the Anderson Estes League in Lee County, Texas, belonging to Jenifer Estes, prepared by the Lee County Land Abstract Company, Giddings, Texas," January 18, 1842.

The Junior Encyclopedia of General Knowledge, edited by Theodore Rowland Entwistle and Jean Cooke, Foreword by Magnus Magnusson, first published in 1978 by Octopus Books Limited, 59 Grosvenor Street, London, WI.

Pictorial History of the American Negro, Foreword by Dr. Charles H. Wesley, January 1, 1933.

The World Book of Estes, Published by Halbert's Family Heritage # 08427.

ACKNOWLEDGEMENTS

Thanks to my sons, Curtis and Jonathan, and also to my loyal and dedicated friend Michele Almodobar, for their enormous support during the memoir writing period.

I am especially grateful to my sister Edna for giving me a tremendous amount of information about the Estes family. Edna, who was born July 26, 1928, passed away 92 years later on her birthday, July 26, 2020. I deeply miss her.

Thanks to my niece Debra Hancock, who has kept in touch with me over the years. She is the only relative in Texas I still have any communication with.

Also, thanks to my neighbor and friend Kevin McBrown, my shopping buddy. Occasionally, I need to go shopping or just get out of the building and go for a ride, and he is always accommodating.

Thanks to Steve Zolno for his help with revising my manuscript.

Finally, many thanks to my friends and neighbors here at the Amistad House; Anastasia Russell, who initially helped me do the research, Josephine Ratnam, editor of the first few chapters, and Pamela

Fadem, who has done an extensive amount of research on Black history. Also thank you, Ethel Murphy for help with editing and introducing me to the publishing company, Regent Press.

PHOTO ALBUM

1. *Abstract of Title* Cover
2. *Abstract of Title* Sample Page
3. *Abstract of Title* Map
4. Ira Lucas Estes (left), my father, 8 years old in 1910
5. My father, Ira Lucas Estes
6. My mother, Ella Jones Estes
7. Family portrait (1944),with Curtis in the bottom row, far left
8. My aunt, Willie Mae Jones
9. My father's nephew Sonny Griffin (left) with my father
10. Bertha Smith, my first cousin (left) and my aunt Amanda Jones (right)
11. First cousin Gladys and her husband Herbert Johnsons
12. Beverly Johnson, my mother's classmate at Prairie View A&M College in the 1930s
13. First cousin Bernice Estes
14. My sister Edna Estes-McNeil
15. George Kerr, Louise Kerr, Curtis L. Estes, Spur, Texas, K-12 School 1955
16. Ella James Estes, at work, Herman Hospital
17. My Sons, Curtis Matthew Estes (left) and Jonathan Lucas Estes (right)
18. Malcolm X Middle School Class of 1973
19. North Berkeley Senior Center

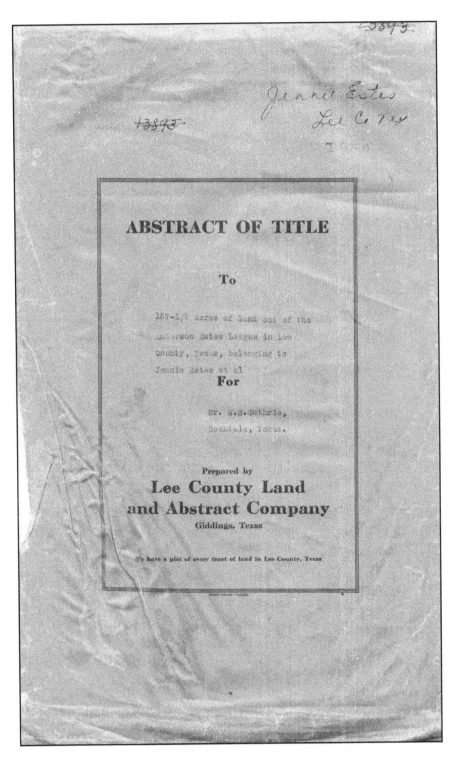

ABSTRACT OF TITLE

To

187-1/2 acres of land out of the
Anderson Estes League in Lee
County, Texas, belonging to
Jennie Estes et al

For

Mr. W.B.Guthrie,
Rockdale, Texas.

Prepared by
Lee County Land
and Abstract Company
Giddings, Texas

We have a plat of every tract of land in Lee County, Texas

Abstract of Title Cover

State of Texas.   * Instrument,   Patent.
                                   * Dated,   January 18th. 1842
            to   * Filed,   March 11th. 1891
                                   * Recorded in Book R page 18 Deed
Anderson Estes   * Records of Lee County, Texas.

No. 764.

In the name of the Republic of Texas,   No. 764.

TO ALL WHOM THESE PRESENTS SHALL COME KNOW YE.

I Sam Houston, President of the Republic aforesaid , by virtue of
the Power vested in me by law, and in accordance with the statutes of
said Republic in such cases made and provided do by these presents
grant to Anderson Estes his heirs and assigns forever One League of
twenty five million square varas. of land, situated and described as
follows. In Washington County, South of the Legua, known on the map
of said County as league M; Beginning at a post oak on the north west
corner of League L. from which a Post Oak bears South 68 East 13 varas;
another Post Oak bears South 37 East 7 varas; Thence South 45 West
Five thousand Nine Hundred & Fifty varas to a post for the North West
corner of this survey, from which a post oak bears South 55 East 5
varas another Post Oak bears North 64 West 15 varas. Thence South 45
E. at 1700 varas a creek at three thousand six hundred and sixty varas
intersected the N.W. boundary line of Blu Hatfield survey at a Post
for the S.W. corner of this survey. from which a Post Oak bears North
24 East 12 varas. Another Post Oak bears North 62 West 14 varas.
Thence North 55 East Six thousand & sixty varas with the North West bou
ary line of Hatifield and T.W.Wards surveys to the south west corn
of league L. Thence North forty five decrees West Four thous
hundred and ten varas with the South West line of said le

2

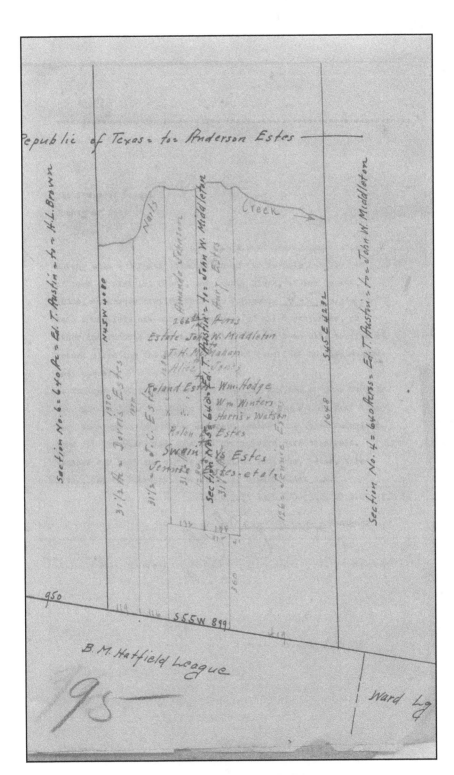

Abstract of Title Map

Ira Lucas Estes (left), my father, 8 years old in 1910

My father Ira Lucas Estes

My mother, Ella Jones Estes

Family portrait (1944)
Curtis is in the bottom row, far left

My aunt Willie Mae Jones

My father's nephew Sonny Griffin (left)
with my father

Bertha Smith my first cousin (left) and my aunt
Amanda Jones (right)

*First cousin Gladys (Doland's daughter) and
her husband Herbert Johnson*

Beverly Johnson, my mother's classmate at
Prairie View A&M College in the 1930s

First cousin Bernice Estes (Doland's daughter)

My sister Edna Estes-McNeil

From left to right:
George Kerr, Louise Kerr, Curtis L. Estes
Spur, Texas, K-12 School 1955

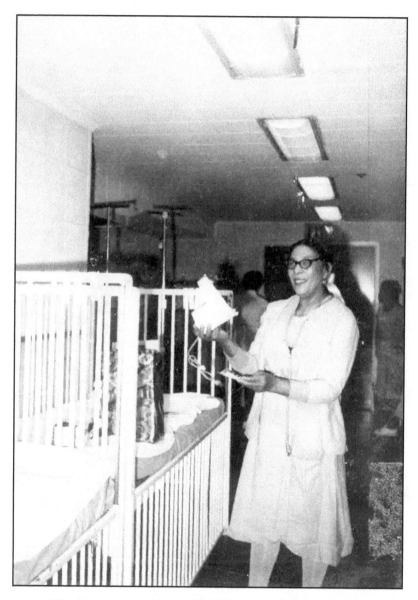

Ella James Estes, at work, Herman Hospital

My Sons, Curtis Matthew Estes (left) and
Jonathan Lucas Estes (right)

Malcolm X Middle School Berkeley Class of 1973

Pool hustlers at North Berkeley Senior Center